D1220371

I do actually have some hobbies, but none worth talking about. Just little things that I dabble in.

In short, *Dragon Ball* is the only thing I can talk to people about.

—Toyotarou, 2020

Toyotarou

Toyotarou created the manga adaptation for the *Dragon Ball Z* anime's 2015 film, *Dragon Ball Z: Resurrection F*. He is also the author of the spin-off series *Dragon Ball Heroes: Victory Mission*, which debuted in *V-Jump* in Japan in November 2012.

Akira Toriyama

Renowned worldwide for his playful, innovative storytelling and humorous, distinctive art style, Akira Toriyama burst onto the manga scene in 1980 with the wildly popular *Dr. Slump*. His hit series *Dragon Ball* (published in the U.S. as *Dragon Ball* and *Dragon Ball Z*) ran from 1984 to 1995 in Shueisha's *Weekly Shonen Jump* magazine. He is also known for his design work on video games such as *Dragon Quest*, *Chrono Trigger*, *Tobal No. 1* and *Blue Dragon*. His recent manga works include *COWA!*, *Kajika*, *Sand Land*, *Neko Majin*, *Jaco the Galactic Patrolman* and a children's book, *Toccio the Angel*. He lives with his family in Japan.

SHONEN JUMP Manga Edition

STORY BY **Akira Toriyama**
ART BY **Toyotarou**

TRANSLATION **Caleb Cook**
LETTERING **Brandon Bovia**
DESIGN **Joy Zhang**
EDITOR **Marlene First**

DRAGON BALL SUPER © 2015 BY BIRD STUDIO, Toyotarou
All rights reserved. First published in Japan in 2015 by SHUEISHA Inc., Tokyo.
English translation rights arranged by SHUEISHA Inc.

The stories, characters and incidents mentioned in this publication are entirely fictional.

No portion of this book may be reproduced or transmitted in any form or by any means without written permission from the copyright holders.

Printed in the U.S.A.

Published by VIZ Media, LLC
P.O. Box 77010
San Francisco, CA 94107

10 9 8 7 6 5 4 3 2 1
First printing, March 2021

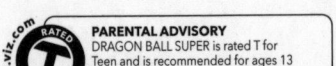

PARENTAL ADVISORY
DRAGON BALL SUPER is rated T for Teen and is recommended for ages 13 and up. This volume contains realistic and fantasy violence.

St. John the Baptist Parish Library
2920 New Hwy. 51
LaPlace, LA 70068

DRAGON BALL SUPER

MERUS'S TRUE IDENTITY

12

STORY BY
Akira Toriyama

ART BY
Toyotarou

CAST OF CHARACTERS

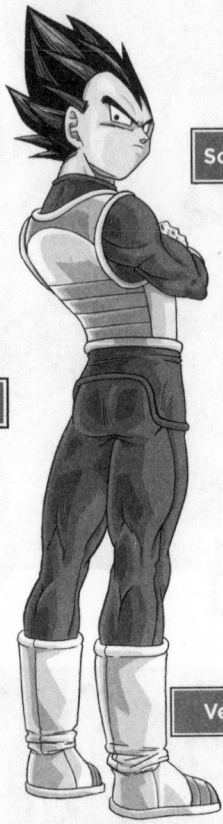

STORY THUS FAR

A long, long time ago, Son Goku left on a journey in search of the legendary Dragon Balls—a set of seven balls that, when gathered, would summon the dragon Shenlong to grant any wish. After a great adventure, he collects them all. Later, he becomes the apprentice of Kame-Sen'nin, fights a number of vicious enemies, defeats the great Majin Boo and restores peace on Earth. Some time passes, and then Lord Beerus, the God of Destruction, suddenly awakens and sets out in search of the Super Saiyan God. Goku, by becoming the Super Saiyan God, manages to stop Beerus from destroying the Earth and starts training under him with Vegeta. After some time, the ancient villain Moro escapes from the Galactic Prison and goes off to search for the Dragon Balls in new Namek, where Goku and the Galactic Patrol confront him. However, Moro's ability to absorb life energy is too much for them, and Moro manages to make his wishes. After retreating, Goku travels to a distant planet to train with Merus, while Vegeta goes to Yardrat to learn about spirit techniques that could defeat Moro. Meanwhile, Moro himself has freed a gang of convicts from the Galactic Prison and is commanding them to attack planets across the galaxy. Now, his evil may threaten Earth as well...

CHAPTER 53 **Saganbo's Galactic Bandit Brigade** 07

CHAPTER 54 **Gohan vs. Seven-Three** 53

CHAPTER 55 **Merus's True Identity** 99

CHAPTER 56 **Warriors of Earth Assemble** 145

DRAGON BALL SUPER

CHAPTER 53: SAGANBO'S GALACTIC BANDIT BRIGADE

GEEZ, WHO DOESN'T HAVE A PHONE IN THIS DAY AND AGE.
AND TENSHINHAN DOESN'T OWN A CELL PHONE, SO WE'VE GOT NO WAY TO REACH HIM.
GOHAN'S AT ONE OF HIS COLLEGE LECTURES, BUT HE'LL SWING BY AFTER THAT.
JACO'S HERE.
SHOOM
SHOULD WE CONTACT YAMCHA?
I TOLD YOU TO GATHER UP ALL THE TOUGHEST WARRIORS!
HEY, BULMA.
WHRRR

DENDE !!
I'M NOT THAT FREE...
KURIRIN WAS THE ONLY ONE WHO COULD COME. HE'S GOT ABSOLUTELY NOTHING ELSE GOING ON.
THE BRAT TAGGED ALONG WHEN I SAID I WAS HEADING FOR EARTH.
YES!
THANK GOOD-NESS YOU'RE SAFE!
IT'S REALLY YOU!
ESCA!
SO IF THERE'S ANY WAY I CAN HELP, PLEASE LET ME KNOW!
I'M READY TO FIGHT FOR PEACE IN THE GALAXY! AND TO RESTORE NAMEK!
...
WAS HE THE ONLY ONE WHO MADE IT?
YEP. YOU THREE ARE THE LAST SURVIVING NAMEK-IANS.

HA HA HA... AS IF YOU LOSERS COULD EVER STAND UP TO MORO.

YOU THREE ARE THE LAST PEOPLE I EXPECTED TO RUN INTO HERE!!
LONG TIME NO SEE, PIP-SQUEAK.

IT'S OBEY OR BE KILLED-- NO THIRD OPTION, Y'HEAR?

PASTA!

ONCE EVERY-THING'S HUNKY-DORY AGAIN...
...YOU'RE HEADED RIGHT BACK TO THE GALACTIC SLAMMER!

UGH, I'VE NEVER MET ANYONE WHO BELONGED IN A CAGE MORE THAN YOU.
MIGHTY KIND OF YOU TO SAY.

YOU LET THEM CONTACT MORO ?!
WHAT ?!
HA HA HA, YOU STILL DON'T GET IT--THE MAIN FORCE IS GONNA SWOOP DOWN TO RESCUE US ANY DAY NOW.
T-TRY LEADING WITH THAT NEXT TIME!
NOD
I'D BETTER ASK HQ TO CONFIRM WHO EXACTLY'S COMING OUR WAY!

NEVER HEARD OF IT... HOW 'BOUT YOU, YUNBA?
"EARTH"? HMM...

IT'S BEEN NOTHING BUT THESE STINKIN' BAR THINGS SINCE WE BUSTED OUTTA PRISON!
OF COURSE!

YOU'VE GOT FOOD ON THE BRAIN AND NOT MUCH ELSE, HUH?

BUT I SURE HOPE IT'S GOT YUMMY TREATS.
NOPE, SHIMO-REKKA.

!
THIRD PLANET FROM ITS STAR, IN THE OUTSKIRTS OF THE NORTHERN SECTOR OF SPACE.

PLANET 4032 GREEN-877.

DATA INDICATES THIS PLANET IS STILL IN THE DEVELOPMENTAL STAGE AND IS OF LITTLE VALUE.
SHOULDA KNOWN YOU'D HAVE THE INTEL, SEVEN-THREE.
HOWEVER, THIS DATA IS FROM BEFORE WE WERE ARRESTED BY THE GALACTIC PATROL. IT COULD BE OUT OF DATE.
PROLLY NOTHING YUMMY THEN...
LITTLE VALUE?
JUST A QUICK STOP!
FINE. WHATEVER.
SOUNDS LIKE A BORING ROCK.
BAH...
NO MORE WAITING!! FIND ANOTHER PLANET FOR A PIT STOP!
GAH! I'M SO HUNGRY!
TCH ...

ALONG WITH OG73-I.
SCANS SUGGEST THAT SHIMOREKKA AND YUNBA ARE ON BOARD.
AGENT JACO! WE HAVE A READ ON THE SHIP CHARTING A COURSE FOR EARTH.
S-SEVEN-THREE IS WITH THEM?!
THEY RAMPAGED AROUND THE GALAXY BEFORE GREAT PAINS WERE TAKEN TO CATCH THEM.
THEY'RE MEMBERS OF AN INFAMOUS BRIGADE OF GALACTIC BANDITS.
ALL THREE ARE SAGAN-BO'S HENCH-MEN.
IS THAT HIS NAME?
WHO THE HECK'S THAT?
...
NO. BY AGENT MERUS.
BY YOU, JACO?

IF YOU SURVIVE, I'LL BE BACK TO RECRUIT YOU LATER.
ON THAT NOTE, I'LL BE OFF.
WHRRR
W-WAIT A SECOND!
OH, SURE!
BUT THE EARTH'S GOT PICCOLO AND GOHAN... WE'LL BE FINE, RIGHT?
BUT TO BE HONEST? YEAH. EXACTLY.
YOU DON'T BEAT AROUND THE BUSH, HUH?
SO YOU'RE SAYING THEY'RE TOO STRONG FOR YOU TO BEAT.
YOU SHOULD STAY AND FIGHT TOO!
LEAVING SO SOON?!
C. CORP.
AT LEAST TELL US THAT BEFORE YOU LEAVE.
WHAT DO WE NEED TO KNOW ABOUT THEM?
I ONLY CAME TO PICK UP THE NEW RECRUITS ANYWAY!
NAH! I'M OUTTA HERE!
YOU'RE THE ONLY ONE WHO KNOWS ANYTHING ABOUT THESE BADDIES! SO YOU'D BETTER HELP US!

SH-SHEESH, FINE.
BUT THEN I'M GONE.

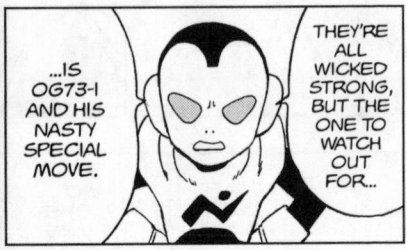
THEY'RE ALL WICKED STRONG, BUT THE ONE TO WATCH OUT FOR..
...IS OG73-1 AND HIS NASTY SPECIAL MOVE.

GRAP
FWK FWK FWK
SHP
SHNK SHNK SHNK
FWAH
SKWEEZ

SHF SHF
SHNK
!!
!!!
SHNK SHNK SHNK

SO THIS ISN'T ABOUT HIJACKING BODIES OR BRAIN-WASHING?
A WHOLE HALF HOUR?
HE CAN STEAL OTHER PEOPLE'S POWERS BY GRABBING THEIR NECKS. THE STOLEN POWERS LAST FOR 30 MINUTES.
A COPY ABILITY?! WHAT DO YOU MEAN?
AN ARTIFICIAL ONE, COOKED UP BY A PLANET WITH ADVANCED TECH AND SCIENCE. SO HE'S GOT NOTHING RESEMBLING NORMAL EMOTIONS OR FEEL-INGS.
WHAT SORT OF BEING IS HE?
SEVEN-THREE'S ALREADY PLENTY STRONG, SO THE ABILITIES HE COPIES JUST GIVE HIM AN EXTRA BOOST.
NAH, NOT LIKE THAT.
HE'S JUST A KILLING MACHINE WHO OBEYS HIS ALLIES' ORDERS.

ZOOM ZOOM
!!
!!
WELL, HOW LONG DO WE HAVE?
THEY'LL BE HERE IN ABOUT TEN DAYS.
ONLY TEN DAYS? I'D BETTER START TRAINING...
HOW ABOUT YOU, PICCOLO?
I NEVER STOP HONING MYSELF EVEN IN THE BEST OF TIMES.

TMP
HUH? WHO'RE THEY?
S-SEV...

THESE THREE ARE THE BANDITS ?!
W-WHAT ?!
SEVEN-THREE!!
H-H-HEY, STOP IN THE NAME OF THE LAW!
WOULD'VE TAKEN DAYS TO GET HERE BY SPACESHIP.
LUCKY US-- THE PLANET WE STOPPED ON WAS HOME TO THESE CRITTERS WHO COULD CREATE WARP PORTALS.
THE MACARENI GANG.
THERE.

DON'T TELL ME YOU WRANGLED THE MACARENI GANG?
NOT A BAD DAY'S WORK!
IT'S JACO.
RIGHT, RIGHT. WHY'RE YOU HERE, GUY?
OH? YOU'RE WITH THE GALACTIC PATROL, YEAH?
DRAWING A BLANK ON YOUR NAME THOUGH...
BE A PAL AND BUST US OUTTA HERE?
YOU SHOWED UP QUICK, SHIMO-REKKA!
AND IF YOU'RE HERE TO SAVE THEM, THINK AGAIN!!
D-DARN RIGHT I DID!!
...
?
I'VE GOT A MESSAGE FOR YOU FROM LORD MORO.
ALIVE AND WELL, HUH?
HEYA, PASTA!

HIS WORDS, NOT MINE.
TRAITORS WHO ACT ON THEIR OWN ARE DISPOSABLE.
SLOOM
!!
GRP

!
NO KILLING ALLOWED IN THE SANCTUARY.
W-WHAT DO YOU WANT?
GET OFFA ME.
AND NO EVILDOERS ALLOWED ON PLANET EARTH.
SO BEGONE !

GAH !!
!!
SHP
PICCOLO !!
ACK!
FWAH
SKWEEZ

WHAP
DO IT, SEVEN-THREE.
W...
TMP
WHAT DID YOU DO...?
O-OH NO.
!!

ZRRG
TCH!
...!
HEH HEH... YOU'VE GOT SOME SWEET MOVES UP YOUR SLEEVE, I GUESS.
YOU LET HIM COPY ALL YOUR ABILITIES !!
WHAT ?!

WO
RMP
KA
POW
WAAAAH!!

JACO !!
ZOOM
AFTER THEM.
ZOOM ZOOM
W-WAIT UP!
GRP

URK!
SHK
NAW, YOU'RE GONNA FIGHT ME.
!!
GUH HUH HUH...
...!!
BWOOF
BWOOF
!
SH

FOR SHORT BURSTS, YEAH.
YOU COULD FLY ALL ALONG?
SKSHH
SORRY... THAT WAS SLOPPY.
YOU JUST HAAAD TO GO AND LET HIM GRAB YOU EVEN AFTER MY WARNING ABOUT HIS ABILITY?
TMP
TMP
MEANING, THAT ONE HE FIRED OFF WAS BASICALLY NO DIFFERENT THAN IF YOU'D DONE IT.
WELL, THE COPIED MOVES ARE JUST AS STRONG AS THE ORIGINALS.
BUT TELL ME HOW BEST TO FIGHT HIM.
RIGHT, I UNDER-STAND.

HERE HE COMES !!
SAME GOES FOR PUNCHES AND KICKS! THEY'RE ALL JUST LIKE YOUR MOVES!
SO I MUST THINK OF IT AS FIGHTING AN EXACT COPY OF MYSELF.
WOR
MP

SHO
OP
GRP
WO
RM
P
GRP

SKF
SKF
SLAM

SKF
SKF
WHAM
WHAM
WHAM
WHAM
WHAM
WHAM

ACK!
YOINK
YOU'VE GOT SOME NERVE, SHIMO-REKKA!
YOU DARE STEAL MY SIDEARM? IT'S AS IMPORTANT AS A GALACTIC AGENT'S LIFE!
OVER HERE, GALACTIC LOSER.
TMP TMP TMP TMP TMP
GIVE IT BACK!!
SHP

MM
BO
OM

SKEEE
FWAH
BWOOM
YOU MIGHT'VE MENTIONED THAT SOONER!
DAMMIT...
FORGOT TO MENTION-- THAT GUY'S GOT INFINITE STAMINA. YOU CAN'T WEAR HIM DOWN.

HOI HOI!!
POW
POW
POW
UGH!
TCH!
WOULDN'T EXPECT SUCH SHARP ATTACKS BASED ON HIS LOOKS!!
TH-THIS GUY...
GAHHH!!
FLAIL
FLAIL
S-SURE THING. CUE BALL NEEDS BACKUP, HUH?
HERCULE! GO AND HELP HIM!

FWSH
HAHH !!
BWOOMP
!
...?
BONG
BONG
!!
SHOOM
FREEZ

KRASH
EEK!
BWOOM
GET IN, EVERY-ONE!
BOM
LET'S FOLLOW THEM!
YOU OKAY DOWN THERE?
C-CUE BALL!
GWAHH!
KAZOOM

RMMMMMBBL
BWOOM

WHOOSH
D-DAMMIT !!
GETTING BEATEN BY MY OWN TECHNIQUES...
JUST TRY TO HOLD OUT!
SORRY, BUT I DON'T THINK I'LL LAST THAT LONG.
HE'LL BE BACK TO NORMAL AFTER 30 MINUTES!
KAWHAP

BWOOM
NNGH...
GAH!
ZRRRG

!
SH
OOM
!!
AH...
AH...
WAS HE BLOWN TO BITS ?!
W-WHERE'D HE EVEN GO?!

OOH, IT'S SON GOKU'S BOY!
!
ARE YOU OKAY, PICCOLO?

...
SO MY DAD AND VEGETA MUST BE OFF WORLD?
BUT WHAT'S GOING ON? WHO ARE THOSE GUYS ?!
I'M SORRY I'M SO LATE.
THANKS FOR THE SAVE, GOHAN.
RIGHT NOW, YOU'RE THE STRONGEST FIGHTER WE'VE GOT ON EARTH.
COPY ?!
I'LL SAVE THE LONG VERSION FOR LATER. FOR NOW, GOHAN, JUST DON'T LET THAT ONE GRAB YOU BY THE NECK, OR ELSE HE'LL COPY YOUR POWERS.
FAR, FAR FROM EARTH, ON AN UN-INHABITED PLANET

POW
SON GOKU AND MERUS TRAIN IN A SPECIAL DIMENSION CUT OFF FROM THE OUTSIDE WORLD, ONE WHERE TIME FLOWS DIFFERENTLY.
WHAM WHAM WHAM WHAM
KATHUD
HFF!
HFF!

I EXPECT YOU WERE IN AN EXTREME CRISIS WHEN IT FIRST ACTIVATED?
FOR SURE. IT WAS A MATTER OF LIFE AND DEATH.
NOW I'M KINDA DOUBTING THAT I ACTUALLY EVER MANAGED TO USE ULTRA INSTINCT...
DARN ...
YOU MEAN, I GOTTA BE PREPARED TO DIE DURING THIS TRAINING?
THEN THE QUICKEST WAY TO ACHIEVE IT AGAIN IS TO REPLICATE THOSE CONDITIONS.
THEN YOU'D BETTER COME AT ME TO KILL.
FINE...
YES. EXACTLY.

PLANET YARDRAT
HEY... HOW MANY MORE DAYS OF THIS?
YOUR SPIRIT IS EVEN LESS STABILE THAN GOKU'S WAS.
FIRST, YOU MUST ACHIEVE BALANCE IN BODY AND MIND.
DAMMIT ...
I'M STARTING TO REGRET EVER COMING TO THIS ROCK...
BY THE WAY, GOKU WAS UP THERE FOR 150 DAYS.
FOR 150 DAYS?!
YOUR BALANCE IS ALL DISRUPTED, AGAIN.
UGH... GRR...

SAGANBO'S GALACTIC BANDIT BRIGADE MEMBER: SHIMOREKKA
SAGANBO'S GALACTIC BANDIT BRIGADE MEMBER: OG73-I
SAGANBO'S GALACTIC BANDIT BRIGADE MEMBER: YUNBA

DRAGON BALL SUPER

CHAPTER 54: GOHAN VS. SEVEN-THREE

SKSHHH
BOOM

BWOOM
WHEF
BWAM BWAM BWAM

VIIIIIIII
SHWEEE
BOOM
BOOM
BOOM
BOOM

BWOOM
GOHAN !!
THERE !!

BWAM
SLAM
!!
SEVEN-THREE !!

I KNOW YOUR MOVES BETTER THAN JUST ABOUT ANYONE, PICCOLO.
WELL DONE, GOHAN!
TMP
AND I'VE GOT MIXED FEELINGS ABOUT YOU BEATING A COPY OF ME THAT EASILY.
RIGHT!
NOW GET OUT THERE AND END THIS.
FWEW
!
FW OO MP

...!
NOW YOU'RE A GIANT, HUH?
BWO OMF

TCH!
FWSH
I'M PRETTY FAMILIAR WITH THAT ONE TOO.
FOOSH
ZOOM

WHAM
TOMP

RRMMMM
TH-THE HECK?!
IT'S THAT OTHER GUY!
SHAKA
SHAKA
!
!
WHAM
POW
POW
...

ZOOSH
TMP
PYEW
PYEW
WOBBL
BOOM
BOOM

ZOOSH
POW

UGH!

!
TH
UD

HUH?
ZOOM

DON'T QUIT ON ME NOW!
HEY!! SEVEN-THREE!

AND **THAT** GUY'S THE ONE WE SHOULDA HAD OUR MAN COPY.

GUESS OUR DATA FOR THIS PLANET WAS SUPER OUTDATED.

WHAT'S GOING ON, SHIMO-REKKA?
TOMP

SHOOM
LISTEN, SEVEN-THREE.
WHATEVER IT TAKES, GET YOUR HAND AROUND THAT GUY'S NECK!
VERY WELL.
WOOF
MP

GRRP
FW SH
OOM
SHOOM
TMP
TMP
DASH
TMP

PIC-COLO!
TMP
DEFINITELY SOMEONE WE CAN COUNT ON. SAME AS ALWAYS.
TOMP
TOMP
YEAH.
GOHAN SHOWED UP, HUH?
SHOOM
SHOOM

...ME...
KA...
SMASH

TMP
TMP
TMP
TMP
TMP
FWACK
HA...
...ME...

!
WORMP
SHAAAH
...!
FIRE IT OFF ANY-WAY, SON GOHAN !!
NOW'S YOUR CHANCE !!
GRRR ...
HE'S OUTTA TIME!!
THE ABILITY WORE OFF!!

W-WAIT, IF HE SHOOTS FROM THERE, THE EARTH'S DONE FOR!
HE'S NO FOOL-- HE'LL DETONATE IT RIGHT AT THE SURFACE.
HAAAA!!
SHOOT!
SEVEN-THREE, USE WHAT YOU'VE GOT IN STOCK!

STOCK ?!
!
FWK
FASH

UGH!
HUH?
W-WHERE'S THE BOOM?
...!!
HMM?
H-HE ATE IT...

HE ATE THE CHI BLAST!
LOOK! MORO !!
HAAH!
GULP
FWP
HE HAD MORO'S POWERS IN STOCK !!
IN STOCK? YOU NEVER SAID ANYTHING ABOUT THAT!
YEAH, WELL, HE CAN SWITCH TO OTHER COPIED ABILITIES, STORING UP TO THREE IDENTITIES AT A TIME!!
WHAT'S THAT MEAN ...?

WHAT NOW?
THIS IS BAD !!
HE'S GONNA ABSORB ENERGY!
TAKE HIM DOWN BEFORE HE CAN !!
TCH!
ZOOM
FLK
BWOOOSH
!!
KRAK KRAK

FWSH
FWK
BWOOSH
GAHH !!
WHAT'S ALL THAT ABOUT ?!
...!!
WE CAN'T GET CLOSE!!
SO Y'SEE, CAPTAIN, WE HAD TO RESORT TO THAT. SORRY.
HMPH... CLOSE ONE, HUH? NEVER THOUGHT WE'D NEED OUR SECRET WEAPON SO SOON.

FINISH UP THERE QUICK AND GET BACK HERE.
...
IS THAT SO?
WHAT? THEY ALREADY MADE USE OF MY COPIED ABILITIES?
APOLO-GIES, LORD MORO.
BUT I DON'T LIKE MY NECK GETTING TOUCHED ALL THE TIME. I DON'T WANT HIM EMPLOYING IT FOR JUST ANYTHING.
COPYING... A USEFUL POWER...
SORRY, THEY WERE SUPPOSED TO BE USED AS A LAST RESORT...
WE CAN CHECK IT OUT FROM HERE, ACTUALLY.
I ASSUME IT'S BEING PUT TO GOOD USE?

PROJECT THE LIVE FEED HERE, QUOITUR.
SURE.
SHIMO-REKKA, SWITCH TO MONITOR MODE.
YOU GOT IT!
HUFF!
HUFF!
HUFF!
BWOOM
F-FEELING DRAINED...

I KNOW.
I AM ONLY TARGETING THESE FOUR.
DANG... HOW'D IT COME TO THIS?
TH-THIS IS THAT ENERGY ABSORPTION!
DON'T ABSORB THE PLANET'S ENERGY. THAT'S ON LORD MORO'S MENU.
TMP
TOMP

IT DOES COME AS A SURPRISE THAT EARTH IS HOME TO BEINGS STRONGER THAN MY GUYS.
RIGHT.

DOES THIS HAVE A TIME LIMIT AS WELL?
YES.
WHICH IS WHY THEY GOTTA END THIS QUICK.

EARTH...? TEN MILLION YEARS AGO IT WAS A PLANET OF MERE MONKEYS.
THEY'VE EVOLVED QUITE A BIT SINCE THEN...

POW POW
SLASH
SMAK
SMA K

TOO BAD FOR YOU, BEING STRONGER DOESN'T ALWAYS NET YOU THE WIN.
GUH HUH HUH...
HEE HEE HEE...
GAAAAH!!
POW POW POW
SLAM
G-GOHAN!!
GAH!!

TCH... UGH!
GWOHH ...
POW POW POW POW
POW POW POW POW
HYAHHH !!
WHAM WHAM WHAM WHAM
HYAH !!
KA WHAK
HUFF
HUFF
SKF SKF
DON'T GET TOO COCKY...

OH... THEM.
THE SAIYANS WHO WERE ON NAMEK.
...GOKU AND VEGETA WILL MAKE SURE YOU GO DOWN.
EVEN IF WE DIE TODAY...
GOKU? VEGETA? WHO'RE THEY?
?
WHAT ABOUT THEM?
TRAIN-ING, YOU SAY?
YOU WON'T GET YOUR WAY, Y'KNOW!
RIGHT NOW THEY'RE TRAINING TO BEAT YOU PUNKS!

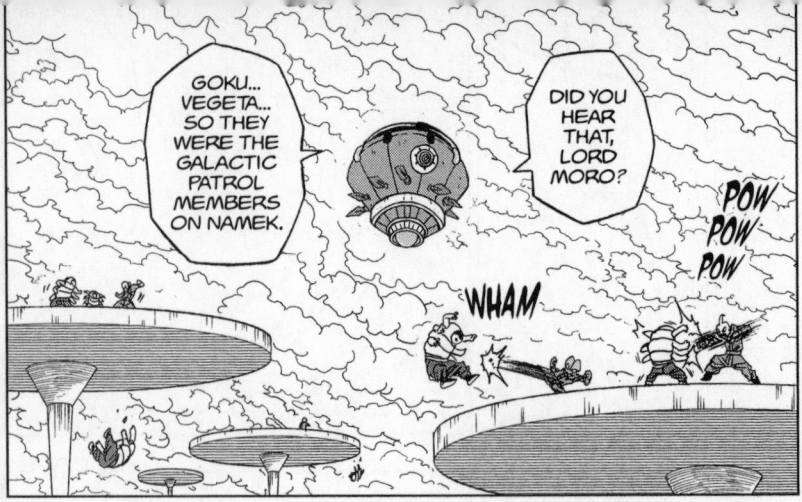
GOKU... VEGETA... SO THEY WERE THE GALACTIC PATROL MEMBERS ON NAMEK.
DID YOU HEAR THAT, LORD MORO?
POW POW POW
WHAM

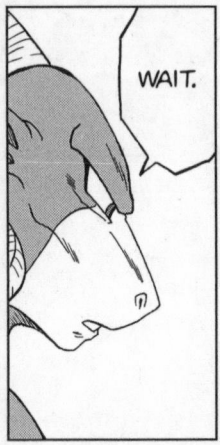
WAIT.

WE'RE TAKING OFF.
PULL EVERYONE BACK FROM THIS PLANET.
SURE.

IF WE LET THEM RUN FREE, IT COULD COME BACK TO BITE US.
WHY NOT JUST GO AND EAT EARTH FIRST?

RIGHT. I THOUGHT THEY JUST TURNED TAIL FOR GOOD BACK THEN... BUT THEY'VE STILL GOT SOME FIGHT LEFT IN THEM. WHO KNEW?

THOSE TWO ARE SUPPOSEDLY TRAINING.

!

...THEY WILL DELIVER ME FAR GREATER ENERGY IF I ONLY WAIT A SPELL.
WHICH MEANS...

THE GALACTIC PATROL NO LONGER POSES A THREAT, SO WE NEED NOT REMAIN HIDDEN FROM THEM.
YOU GOT IT.

ONCE THE ONES CALLED GOKU AND VEGETA RETURN WITH MORE ENERGY THAN EVER, I SHALL CONSUME THEM AND THEIR PRECIOUS EARTH.

...TELL THOSE THREE TO RETREAT FROM EARTH.
FOR NOW...

HUH?

YUNBA, SEVEN-THREE--CAPTAIN'S ORDERING US TO SAY BYE-BYE TO THIS ROCK AND GET BACK TO THE MAIN FORCE.
YOU HEAR THAT, BOYS?
HUH? SURE, OKAY.
HUH? WHY?
!
FZZL
SON GOKU AND VEGETA.
TMP
... AFTER THOSE SAIYANS SHOW UP.
WE'RE GONNA DO THIS JOB LATER ...

YEAH. THOSE TWO.
BAH!
THUD
HUFF!
HUFF!
HUFF!
BORING ...
YOU PEOPLE GOT OFF EASY.
...!
BUT WHY...? WHAT'S GOING ON?
LORD MORO'S GONNA COME AND GOBBLE UP THOSE SAIYANS HIMSELF.
SO THE BIG BOSS IS COMING HERE?
YEP. THEN YOU FOOLS AND THIS PLANET ARE DONE FOR.
BETTER TELL YOUR SAIYAN PALS TO GET BACK HERE, 'KAY?

WE'LL BE BACK IN GALACTIC CYCLE 7, SO DON'T EVEN THINK OF RUNNING.
...!
Y'SEE, THIS PLANET'S TECH IS TOTALLY PRIMITIVE, SO IT'S GONNA TAKE TIME! YOU GOTTA WAIT UNTIL AT LEAST CYCLE 8!
BUT THEY'LL NEVER MAKE IT BACK BY CYCLE 7, SHIMO-REKKA!
IN EARTH TIME, ABOUT 20 DAYS.
H-HOW LONG DOES THAT GIVE US?
PHEW!
THAT LONG? FOR REAL?
I'LL LET LORD MORO KNOW.
FINE.

WOOM
KACHK
SKWEEZ
POP
SHOOP
LATER.
TMP

KOFF KOFF
KOFF
GOHAN! YOU OKAY?
...
WE'RE SAFE FOR NOW... I THINK?
AND TAKE IT EASY. DENDE CAN PATCH YOU RIGHT UP. HIM, OR A SENZU BEAN.
SORRY, I LET THEM GET AWAY.
DON'T SWEAT IT! WE WOULD'VE REALLY BEEN IN TROUBLE WITHOUT YOU HERE.
NICE GOING JACO!
YOU BOUGHT US AN EXTRA MONTH AND THEN SOME?
IN TWO MONTHS.
SO WHEN ARE THEY ACTUALLY RETURNING, JACO?

...
I MEAN, I CAN'T GO DYING BEFORE THAT ONE ANIME MOVIE COMES OUT NEXT MONTH.
YOU'RE ALIVE!!
GUYS !!
BUL-MA!
ZOOM
NEWS OF MORO'S IMPENDING TRIP TO EARTH REACHED MERUS VIA GALACTIC PATROL HQ.
UNDER-STOOD. WE WILL TRAVEL TO EARTH IN TWO MONTHS' TIME.
HOW-EVER, THE COUNTDOWN BEGAN FOR THIS GRAVE THREAT'S NEXT VISIT.
AND SO, EARTH WAS SAFE FROM DANGER FOR THE TIME BEING.

IT SEEMS ALL IS WELL, THOUGH. THANK GOODNESS AGENT JACO WAS THERE FOR THEM.
GOTCHA! BUT THEY SAID THE BAD GUYS ARE GONNA COME BACK?
YES.
MORO'S PALS SHOWED UP ON EARTH?!
HUH ?!
IT GIVES US SIX MONTHS IN HERE. I FEEL SORRY FOR THE PLANETS THAT WILL BE SACRIFICED IN THE MEANTIME, BUT ASSURING MORO'S CAPTURE WHEN THE TIME COMES IS OUR TOP PRIORITY.
TWO MONTHS... THAT'S MORE TIME THAN WE THOUGHT, HUH?
YES.
MY BELLY'S FULL, SO LET'S GET RIGHT BACK TO IT!
WELL, FINE!
THAT MEANS MY TRAINING'S GOTTA PAY OFF, OR ELSE.

HUH? WHIS SAID THE SAME THING.
I CAN EAT, OR NOT EAT. IT'S ALL THE SAME TO ME.
I JUST REALIZED... I'VE NEVER SEEN YOU EAT. DON'TCHA EVER GET HUNGRY?

FWP

THE FOOD HERE'S KINDA MEH.
IF IT'S THE SAME TO YOU, THEN MAYBE I WON'T EAT EITHER.

DASH
DASH

APOLO-GIES FOR THE SUDDEN REQUEST.
WHIS?
NOW, HOW CAN I HELP YOU...
SO VERY SORRY TO MAKE YOU WAIT.

I PRESUME YOU ARE AWARE THAT OUR UNIVERSE IS ONCE AGAIN IN DISCORD?
GRAND PRIEST.
WELL, WHAT BUSINESS DID YOU HAVE WITH ME?
I AM DEEPLY ASHAMED FOR IT.
UNIVERSE 7 IS CERTAINLY A RESTLESS ONE.
IT SEEMS THAT WAY.
JUST SO.
I WOULD NEVER. WE ANGELS MUST MAINTAIN NEUTRALITY, SIDING WITH NEITHER GOOD NOR EVIL.
THEN WHAT WOULD YOU ASK OF ME?
I DON'T SUPPOSE YOU INTEND TO ASK FOR YOUR UNIVERSE TO BE SAVED?
YOU ARE AWARE, THEN?
THE MATTER OF MERUS, I SUPPOSE.
THERE IS SOMETHING I WISH TO CONFIRM CONCERNING OUR ANGEL LAWS...

SAGANBO'S
GALACTIC BANDIT
BRIGADE LEADER:
SAGANBO

DRAGON BALL SUPER

CHAPTER 55: MERUS'S TRUE IDENTITY

HIS ENLISTING IN THE GALACTIC PATROL SEEMED A DECENT CHOICE, AS IT WOULD ALLOW HIM TO OBSERVE THE SIDE OF GOOD AND VIRTUE, BUT, ALAS...
BEYOND THAT SINGLE LAW, THERE ARE NO RESTRICTIONS ON WHAT WE CAN OR CANNOT DO.
WE ANGELS MUST ALWAYS ACT IM-PARTIALLY.
INDEED.
ANY FURTHER INVOLVE-MENT WOULD MAKE HIM IN VIOLATION OF OUR CODE.
JUST SO.
HE SEEMS TO HAVE GAINED A BIAS?
MEAN-ING?
...
MIGHT YOU ALLOW ME TO COLLECT MERUS AND DEAL WITH HIM ON MY OWN?
GRAND PRIEST.
...I SHALL HAVE TO END MERUS'S TENURE IN THE MORTAL REALM.
AS HE IS PUSH-ING THE LIMIT ...

St. John the Baptist Parish Library
2920 New Hwy. 51
LaPlace, LA 70068

GO ON.
I LEAVE MERUS IN YOUR CARE.
MUCH OBLIGED.
BUT DO KEEP A CLOSE EYE ON THAT ONE.
UNDER-STOOD.

TROUBLE-MAKER OR NOT...
...I DO NOT WISH TO LOSE AN ANGEL.

PLANET YARDRAT
KNNNT
KNNNT

WITH NO WAY TO COMMUNICATE, IRICO AND VEGETA COULDN'T RECEIVE UPDATES.
YARDRAT FALLS OUTSIDE OF THE GALACTIC PATROL'S JURISDICTION.
WHAT'S GOING ON OUT IN THE GALAXY...? I SURE HOPE EVERYONE'S OKAY...
DARN... I STILL CAN'T GET AHOLD OF HQ.
KZZZT
HMM?
WAIT. THAT SHIP...
KNOCK

TMP
TMP
HUP!
HUP!
TMP

HEF
THUD
HEF
HEF
HEF
THOOM
HEF
HEF
KAKAR-ROT AND I ARE NOT CUT FROM THE SAME CLOTH.
OF COURSE.
YOUR SPIRIT IS NOW MORE POLISHED THAN GOKU'S, AND YOU MANAGED IT IN NO TIME.
MM, WON-DERFUL SPIRIT POWER.
AT LAST.
NOW, TO BEGIN TEACHING YOU OUR ABILITIES.

WAS THAT...
...A HEALING TECH-NIQUE?
ONE OF ELDER PYBARA'S SIGNATURE MOVES. PRETTY GREAT, HUH?

FWK
!
SHAH

AND I CAN LEARN TO PERFORM SUCH A MOVE?

FIRST, THE MOST FUNDA-MENTAL BASICS-- I WILL TEACH YOU INSTANT TELEPOR-TATION.

TCH...
WHAT CAN I DO AT THIS POINT THEN?

HA HA HA, DON'T GET AHEAD OF YOUR-SELF.
THAT'S HIGH-LEVEL STUFF, AND YOU'RE NOT THERE JUST YET.

INSTANT TELEPOR-TATION IS ONLY THE BASICS?

KABOOM
I-I'M SENSING WICKED SPIRITS ON OUR PLANET!!
RMMMBL
WHAT THE--?
!
YIKES... WE'VE GOT SOME UN-PLEASANT GUESTS.
ZOOM
VEGETA !!

WAIT, VEGE-TA.
DUN

THEY'VE MADE IT OUT THIS FAR?
TCH...

MORO'S GOONS ARE HERE!!
IT'S BAD!

BE MINDFUL OF HOW YOU WIELD THAT POWER, OKAY?
YOU'RE STILL IN TRAINING.

WHAT NOW?

TRY TO KEEP UP, IRICO!
SHOOM

?

DAMMIT !!
KABOOM
!

BWOOM
HEH HEH HEH ...
GAH!
KRAK
TMP
WHO MIGHT THIS BE?
ONE THAT IS SURE TO PLEASE LORD MORO.
A LOVELY PLANET, BRIMMING WITH ENERGY...

LORD MORO OUGHT TO KNOW ABOUT THIS...

MORO WON'T BE MAKING A MEAL OF THIS PLANET.
THAT'S YUZUN--ONE OF SAGANBO'S MINIONS.

HO HO HO! SO YOU'VE FLED ALL THE WAY TO THIS ROCK?
OH, YOU ARE... YES, THE GALACTIC PATROL MEMBER FROM NAMEK!

NOT ON MY WATCH.

BWOOOM

HUH?!
BWOOM
SHOOM
W...
WHAT THE ?!

BWOOSH
RMMMBL
WITH NO WARNING ...?
H-HOW DARE YOU?!
RMBL

KNOCK THAT OFF! DON'T GO WRECKING OUR PLANET!
FWK
FWK
WHAT WAS THAT ...?
W...
BEFORE YOUR TRAINING HERE, YOUR BODY AND SPIRIT WERE SO OFF-BALANCE THAT YOU COULDN'T PROJECT YOUR OWN POWER VERY WELL.
WHAT?
CARE TO EX-PLAIN?
GOOD THING NOBODY ACTUALLY LIVES IN THIS CITY, BUT STILL.
YOU JUST WIT-NESSED YOUR OWN NASCENT POWER.
BY LEAPS AND BOUNDS.
SURE HAVE.
MEANING I'VE ALREADY GROWN STRONGER SINCE I ARRIVED ...?

YOU OKAY, BOSS YUZUN?
D-DAMMIT ...
!
LIKE I SAID, YOU GOTTA BE MINDFUL OF THAT POWER.
R-RIGHT !!
FIGHT BACK!!
WHAT'RE YOU FOOLS STARING AT?!
ZOOSH
ZOOSH

THUD
THUD
UGH...
TWITCH
TWITCH
!

NOW I'M MAD!
!
NWAHH...
...GET AWAY WITH THIS...
YOU WON'T...
BW
AK

GUH HUH HUH ...
NOW THAT I'VE TRANSFORMED, YOU'RE DONE FOR.
!!!
POP POP
MAKE MORE CLONES!
EEK!
POP
THIS SHOULDN'T BE A PROBLEM.
YEAH? I'VE SEEN PLENTY LIKE HIM.
I-I'VE NEVER SEEN A TRANS-FORMA-TION BEFORE ...
!
I'LL SPARE LORD MORO THE TROUBLE OF KILLING YOU...
THEN WHY DON'T YOU TRY ME?

TRY YOU? I BELIEVE I JUST DID.
SKF
SKF
SORRY, I DIDN'T QUITE CATCH THAT. WHO EXACTLY ...
...WILL YOU BE KILLING ...?

GRAHHH!!
KRMBL
SLAM

WHAM
SKE
SKE
SKE
TOMP

SKF SKF SKF
KUNK
SHUP
GRP

HE'S LIFTING THE WHOLE BUILDING ?!
RMMMBL
STRAIN
GRAHHH !!

FWP
FLK
TAP

THOOM

FWOOSH
NOT A CHANCE ...

DOOM

YOU'RE NO MATCH FOR ME, SO JUST STOP.
THIS IS FUTILE.

HE'S PUMPED IT FULL OF ENERGY TO HARDEN IT.
FWOOOM
YOU'RE DONE FOR!!
HA
HHH
TMP

!!
WH
AK
SH
FLKR
ZOOM
FWOP
GAHHH
!!

KA
POW
WHAM
ARGH...
GAH ...
GUH ...
SLAM
KRASH KRASH
SKF SKF SKF

TCH...
I CAN'T ALLOW YOU TO RUN BACK TO MORO.
BUT IF YOU SURRENDER AND RETURN TO THE GALACTIC PRISON, I WON'T HAVE TO KILL YOU.
KRMBL
I TOLD HIM NOT TO WRECK THE PLACE ...
WHOA !!
OH? THAT SURE GOT YOU WORKED UP.
COULD THAT BE THE PLANET YOU CALL HOME?
VOOM
IT'S A PLACE CALLED EARTH.
HMPH! DON'T YOU FRET-- LORD MORO'S NEXT TARGET ISN'T THIS PLANET.
?
WHAT ?!
!

ANY-HOW, I'LL BE TAKING MY LEAVE NOW.
DID I HEAR THAT RIGHT? EARTH'S ON THE MENU?!
TMP
SHWP
SO THAT SCUM HAS SET HIS SIGHTS ON EARTH, HAS HE?!
KAZOOSH
TMP
TOMP

ZOOOM
BYE!!
HA HA HA!
FWP
TH-THAT JERK!!
HYAH HA HA HA HA HA!!

EEP!
KRASH
KABOOM
KRMBL
KRMBL
AH... AHH...
BWOOM
!!
W- WHAT THE HECK?!
HMPH!
SO HE KILLED HIMSELF.

HUH?
HOW CAN YOU TELL?
NO. EARTH REMAINS UNTOUCHED FOR NOW.
W-WHAT NOW, VEGETA?! SHOULDN'T WE HURRY BACK TO EARTH?!
AH.
...

INSTANT TELE-PORTATION WON'T CUT IT. I NEED A TECHNIQUE CAPABLE OF BRINGING DOWN MORO.
I'M SHORT ON TIME, PYBARA.
HONING YOUR SPIRIT ALLOWS YOU TO SENSE OTHER SPIRITS--EVEN ONES FAAAR, FAR AWAY.
FWK

THERE'S NO POINT AT ALL IF HE WON'T MAKE IT IN TIME.
HUH?
FINE.
AND YOU CAN'T GO MESSING AROUND WITH THE ORDER THE LESSONS COME IN!
THAT'S "ELDER PYBARA" TO YOU!
WHOA THERE, BUDDY! SHOW HIM SOME RESPECT!

THAT ONE CALLED VEGETA.
I SEE. HE TRULY HAS GROWN MORE POWERFUL.
WHAT? IT CAN'T BE.
ON THE PLANET YUZUN VENTURED TO, YES. THOUGH YUZUN IS NOW DEAD.
YOU FOUND HIM?
!
IN THAT CASE, I SHALL STOCK UP AND REACH THE UPPER LIMITS OF MY POWER BEFORE TRAVELING TO EARTH.
HEH HEH HEH... WHAT A DELIGHTFUL DEVELOPMENT.
WHEN HE TRANSFORMS, HE'S SUPPOSED TO BE UNBEATABLE...

MEANWHILE, GOKU AND VEGETA'S TRAINING ALSO PROGRESSED, UNTIL, AT LAST, TWO MONTHS HAD PASSED.

LEADING UP TO HIS ATTACK ON EARTH, MORO CONTINUED TO DEVOUR PLANETS THROUGHOUT THE GALAXY.

TIME IS NEARLY UP.
LET US SPAR ONCE MORE BEFORE TAKING OFF FOR EARTH.
SOUNDS GOOD.
I'LL JUST HAFTA USE EVERY-THING I'VE LEARNED IN HERE.

I WON'T HOLD BACK EITHER.
RMMBL
SKF
SKF
WBOM
WBOM
WBOM
RMMBL
BWOOM

FWOOP
H-HEY.
WE'RE OUTSIDE AGAIN!
...
WHAT?

THAT'S ...
...QUITE ENOUGH.

FSSH

B...
BROTH-ER.

HMM?
BROTH-ER?

HUH?
IT'S YOU, WHIS!

SO YOU CAUGHT WIND OF WHAT I WAS UP TO?

IT HAS BEEN AGES, MERUS.

I'M AFRAID THERE ARE NO SECRETS...
...BETWEEN ANGELS.
ANGELS ?!
I KNEW YOU WERE WEIRD, BUT YOU'RE AN ANGEL, MERUS?
YES.
TRAINING CAN ONLY BE JUST THAT-- TRAINING.
CLASHING AGAINST EACH OTHER AT FULL STRENGTH CONSTITUTES A BATTLE.
APOLO-GIES.
EVEN MORE EGREGIOUS ...
...WAS YOUR PLAN TO TRAVEL TO EARTH AND DO BATTLE AGAINST MORO.
!
Y-YOU KNEW...

I APOLOGIZE FOR KEEPING IT FROM YOU...
THAT EXPLAINS A LOT, MERUS.
WHAT HAPPENS IF YOU GUYS DO FIGHT?
BUT WAIT ...
JUST SO.
OHH, RIGHT. ANGELS AREN'T ALLOWED TO FIGHT EXCEPT IN TRAINING, RIGHT?
...WITHOUT A TRACE.
ANGELS WHO BREAK OUR CODE ARE ERADICATED ...
THERE IS NO WAY AROUND THIS TRUTH--SUCH IS THE NATURE OF ANGELS.
IT IS THE ONLY MEANS BY WHICH AN ANGEL CAN BE REMOVED FROM EXISTENCE.
I THOUGHT ANGELS COULDN'T DIE!
ERADI-WHAT?! LIKE, POOF?!
HUH?

UNDER-STOOD.
FLK
HENCEFORTH, I WILL BE RESPONSIBLE FOR YOU.
...
YEESH...
ON THAT NOTE, I'VE COME TO INFORM YOU THAT YOUR TIME IN THE MORTAL REALM IS OVER, MERUS.
MERUS...
FWOOM
BE GRATEFUL THAT I'M NOT DRAGGING YOU RIGHT BACK TO THE GRAND PRIEST.
TAP

FLK
GOKU...
I'M ONLY SORRY I COULDN'T SEE THIS THROUGH WITH YOU.
TAP
FWOOM
!
I'LL FIGURE SOME-THING OUT.
SURE.
I HAVE FAITH THAT YOU WILL DEFEAT MORO.
IT'S BACK TO THE HEAVENLY REALM WITH YOU.
YES.

TWNKL
KAZOOSH
THANKS, MERUS.
UNTIL NEXT TIME, GOKU.

COME BAAACK, WHIS!!
WAAAIT!! I CAN'T DO IT!!
HOLD UP! I GOTTA PILOT THAT THING BACK TO EARTH MYSELF?!
ANYHOO... BETTER GET MYSELF BACK TO EARTH.
...

SAGANBO'S
GALACTIC BANDIT
BRIGADE MEMBER:
YUZUN

DRAGON BALL SUPER

CHAPTER 56: WARRIORS OF EARTH ASSEMBLE

EARTH
...

FWP
TMP
SHUV
TMP TMP TMP

HEY, NEW RECRUITS!! LOOK SHARP!
CRUD... WHY'D THEY GOTTA PUT ME IN CHARGE OF EARTH? OF ALL THE ROTTEN LUCK.
IT'S FINALLY MY CHANCE TO SHINE!
IT'S BEEN SO LONG... I HOPE I CAN STILL FIGHT.
...
WE'RE PRETTY MUCH THE VETS OF PROTECTING THE EARTH...
TCH! NEW RECRUITS?

SHWP

ARE GOKU AND VEGETA STILL NOT HERE, JACO?

YEAH. WON'T BE LONG NOW.
IT'S FINALLY TIME.

...I'M SURE THEY'LL SHOW.
BUT GIVEN THE BEEF THOSE TWO HAVE WITH MORO ...

HUH?! THAT'S BAD!
I SENT GOKU A HEADS-UP, BUT WE'VE GOT NO CLUE WHERE VEGETA IS.

VRRRM
BOO!
HE'S BEEN FAST ASLEEP SINCE HIS LAST BATTLE.
SO GLAD YOU'RE OKAY, PAL...
ZZZ
ZZZ

GALACTIC PATROL OR NOT, YOU'LL BE ANSWERING TO ME IF YOU TRY KIDNAPPING BOO AGAIN!
S-SORRY ABOUT THAT.
WHAT DOES MORO'S SPACE-SHIP LOOK LIKE?
A BIG MOTHER-SHIP SHAPED LIKE A TOP WITH LOTS OF LITTLE SCOUT SHIPS.
LIKE THAT ONE?

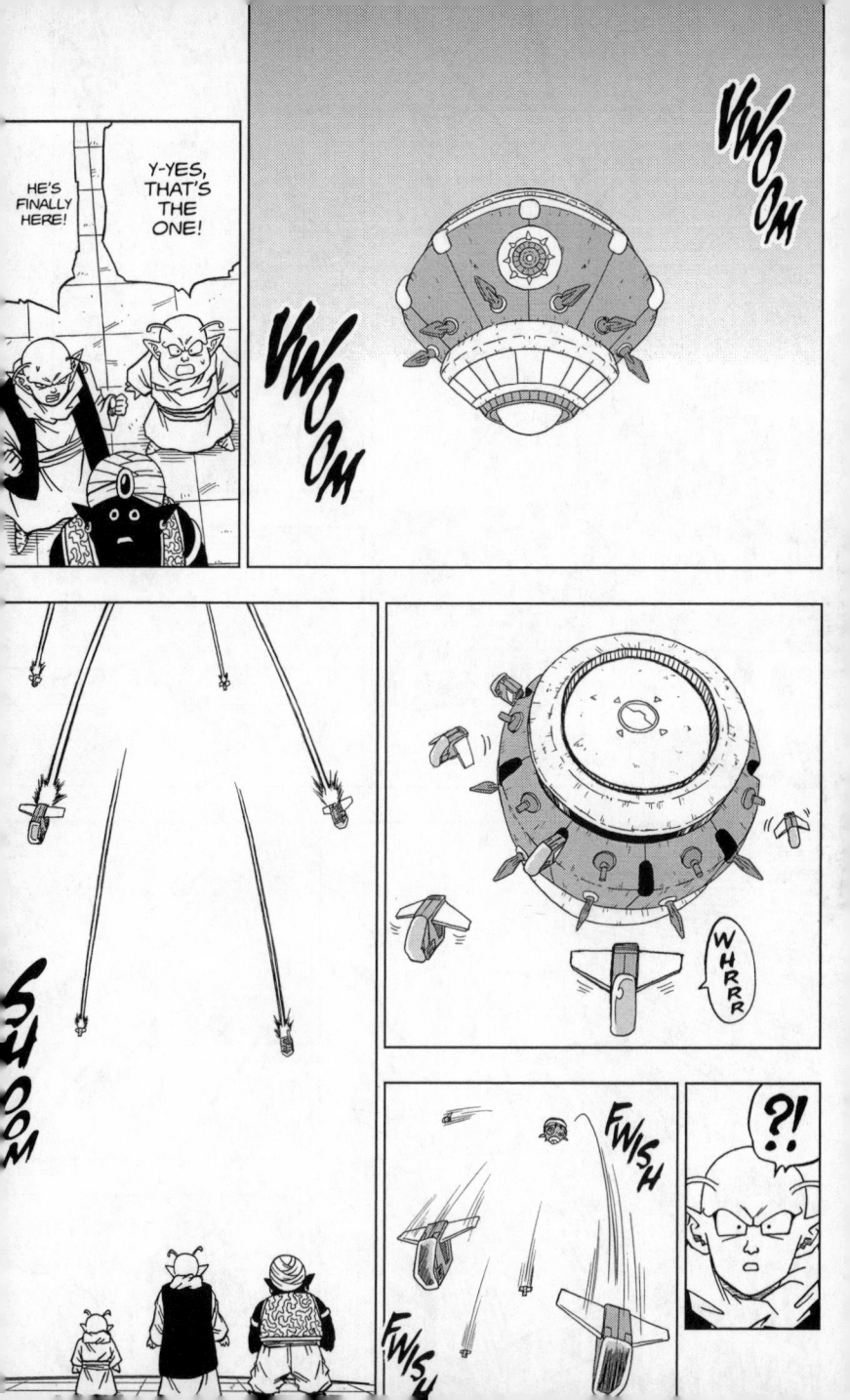
HE'S FINALLY HERE!
Y-YES, THAT'S THE ONE!
VWOOM
VWOOM
SWOOM
WHRRR
FWISH
FWISH
?!

ZOOSH
SHOOM
SHOOM
HUH?
WHAT THE --?
PEW PEW P
HMM?
WHAT'S THAT?

W-WHAT IN THE WORLD ...?!
BOOM
!!
!
TOMP
FLIP
!!
WH ...
WHO THE HECK ARE YOU?!
HAND OVER ALL YOUR TREASURES!

ZOOSH
BWOOOSH
SLAM
SLAM
FWAH
WH-WHO'S THAT ?!
!!

THE BADDIES'RE FLYING OFF TO EVERY CORNER OF THE WORLD!
PICCOLO! WHAT'S HAPPENING?
BEFORE THE FULL-SCALE ATTACK, THEY'RE PROBABLY PLANNING TO ROB THE EARTH OF ALL ITS TREASURES!!
DANG IT!
!
!!
SHP
TMP
CAREFUL OUT THERE! YOU'RE UP AGAINST VICIOUS CRIMINALS!
YUP!
!
OFF WE GO, KURIRIN!
OH... RIGHT.
TCH... OF COURSE!
...WHILE YOU BOYS FIGHT THE BIG BOSS.
LET'S HANDLE THOSE FAR-FLUNG CONVICTS...

TMP
TMP
I'LL HEAD THIS WAY.
YEAH!
LET'S GO, CHAOZU.
KACHK
KACHK
BACK THEM UP!
SPLIT INTO TEAMS AND SUPPORT EARTH'S WARRIORS!
STP
STP STP STP
VWOOM
VWOOM

WE'RE HERE TO HELP, AGENT YAMCHA!
GREAT! FOL-LOW ME!
ZOOSH
ZOOSH
DOWN THERE.
HERE WE GO.
KRAK
KAPOW

SHWP
!
KRAK
HAHH!!
SHWP

TMP
I'M NOT THE SAME MAN AS BE-FORE!
I'VE BEEN TRAIN-ING HARD!
FWAP
YOU AGAIN?
HNNGH...
FINE BY ME. LET'S SETTLE THIS NOW.
GUH HUH HUH ...

ZOOM
...

YUNBA! WE DON'T GIVE A CRAP ABOUT THIS DUEL OF YOURS, SO WE'RE GONNA GO WRECK SOME OTHER PLACE.
SURE. GO ON, THEN.

DASH
DASH
DASH

KURI-RIN...
Y'CAN'T GO RELYING ON YOUR OLD MASTER FOR EVERY-THING. I'M BETTING YOU CAN HANDLE THIS CHUMP ALONE.

MUTEN RŌSHI... THIS GUY'S WAY FASTER THAN HE LOOKS, SO LET'S RUSH HIM TOGETHER!

MEAN-WHILE, I'LL GO WRANGLE THOSE NASTY BABES.
♪
BOING
HUH?!

!

KA-POW
I AIN'T WAITING AROUND!
RMMBL
HAHH!!
POW
POW
POW
OWWW!
DARN YOU!!

HANG IN THERE, GUYS...
THERE'RE FIGHTS STARTING ALL OVER THE PLANET...
WE'VE GOT COMPANY TOO.
ALONE THIS TIME?
YOU WISH.
TMP

FWUNK
WHA--
HUH?
ZRM
!!
W-WHEN DID HE--

TCH !!
ZRM
ZRM
YOU PEOPLE ARE DUMB AS EVER, I SEE.
THAT MOVE CAME COURTESY OF AN INVISIBLE RACE.
I-IDIOT! YOU DROPPED YOUR GUARD AGAIN!
ANY TRAINING YOU MIGHT'VE DONE? ALL TOTALLY WORTHLESS NOW.
DAM-MIT!!
SINCE SEVEN-THREE COPIES YOU THE WAY YOU ARE RIGHT NOW.

PIC-COLO'S TECH-NIQUE AGAIN!
SHWP
TMP
FWAH
TMP
YOUR OWN MOVE'S GONNA SEND YOU TO HELL!!
ZHOOM

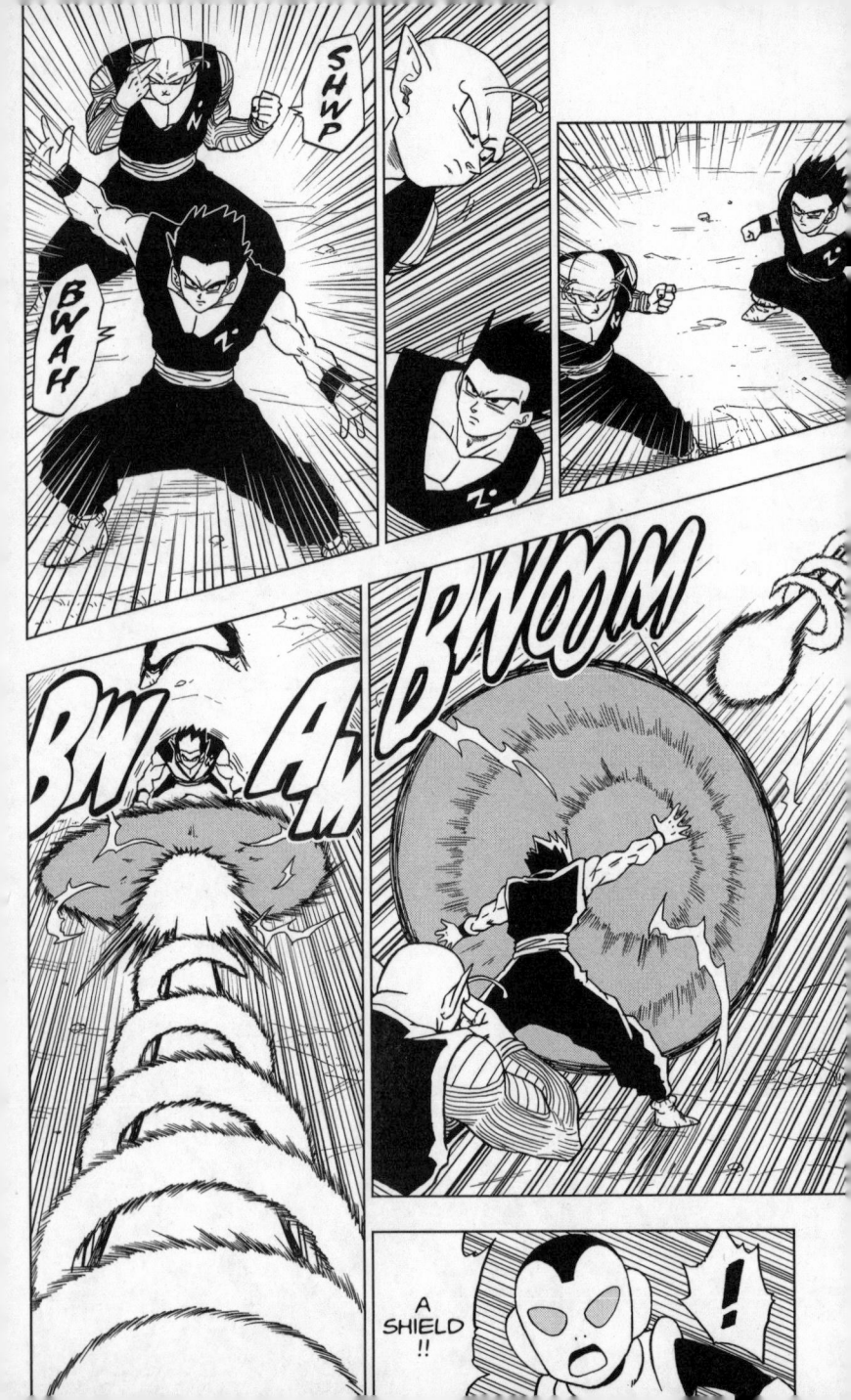
SHWP
BWAH
BWOOM
BW
AH
A SHIELD !!
!

KAZHOOM
KAZHOOM KAZHOOM
FWRL
WHRRRRI

EAT THIS...
LIGHT OF DEATH !!
ZHOOM
ZRRRG

ZOOSH!!!
ZHOOM
KA
FWOO
SH

LOOK, TEN...
THAT'S PICCOLO'S! THE FIGHTING MUST'VE STARTED BACK THERE TOO.
FWOOSH

EVEN WITH INFINITE STAMINA, IT'S NOT LIKE HE CAN RECOVER IMMEDI-ATELY.

KRK KRK
SPLORCH
B-BUT HOW?!
HOW'S THIS HAPPENING?!
BRGL BRGL
WE WERE TOTALLY READY FOR HIM TO COPY OUR ABILITIES.
RRIP
SWITCH OVER TO HIM!
SEVEN-THREE, THAT ONE GUY IS STRONGER.
VERY WELL.
HMPH! SOUNDS LIKE A BLUFF TO ME.

FWK
HYMM
SH
BOOM
GOT IT!
LET'S MOVE!

HUMM HUMM
TCH!
PEW PEW PEW PEW
GOHAN!
PEW
ZOOM

TMP
TMP
BOOM
PEW PEW PEW

PEW
PEW
PEW
TMP
TMP
BOOM
TMP

AK

SPLOOSH
GOOD GOING, GOHAN !!
OF COURSE! COMBO MOVES !!
SEVEN-THREE CAN ONLY USE ONE SET OF POWERS AT A TIME...
...SO THERE'S NO WAY HE CAN DODGE ATTACKS FROM A DUO!
TH-THAT CAN'T BE!
WE'LL NEVER LOSE TO SOME COPYCAT.
SPLOOSH

SEEMS LIKE GOHAN AND PICCOLO'S TRAINING IS PAYING OFF.
UGH!
YOU LOOKED SO FREAK-IN' WEAK...
DAM-MIT...
GAH!
ACTUALLY, I'M ONE OF THE THREE STRONG-EST EARTH-LINGS AROUND.
AW, YOU THINK?

POW
POW
POW
ZOOSH
RAHHHH!!
ZOOM
POW
WHAK
WHAK
...
RIGHT!
BETTER ROUND THEM UP WHILE YOU CAN.
URRGH ...
THUD
THUD
TMP

KASHOOM
KASHOOM

I'M SENSING MORE RAMPAGING CONVICTS THAT WAY... LET'S HURRY!

ZOOM
RMMMBL

HAHHHH!!
VNN VNN

FLASH ...
...OF DEATH !!
SHOO
ZHOOM

WHRR
WHRRRL
RMMB
AAAH

KA BOOM
BRGL
BRGL
BRGL
BRGL
RMMMMBL
DID WE GET HIM ?!
HFF!
HE'LL RESORT TO MORO'S POWER AGAIN...
IF WE DON'T FINISH HIM OFF... HE'LL...
NO, NOT YET!
...

TMP
TMP
IT'LL BE FOR NOTHING IF WE END UP DEAD!!
C'MON! JUST USE IT ALREADY, SEVEN-THREE.
TMP
FWK

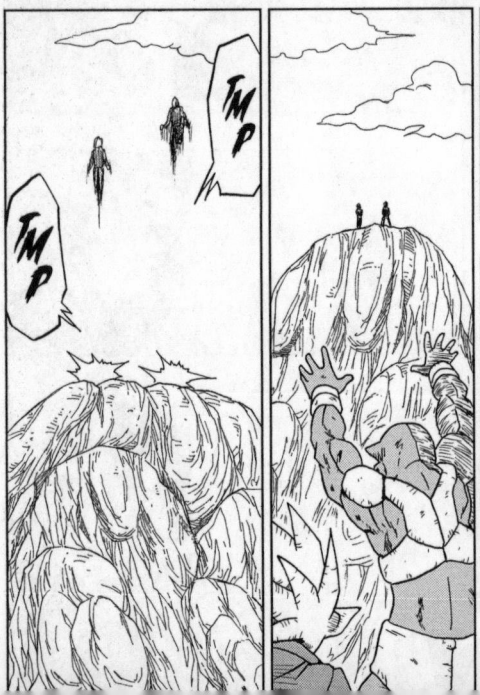
TMP
TMP

GET THEM! DRAIN THEIR ENERGY TILL THEY'RE DRY!!

FWP

ZOOM
WHAM
SLAM
SLAM
TMP
TMP

THEY SAID HE'S GOT NO EMOTIONS... SO YEAH, PROBABLY.
WHICH ONE'S THAT SEVEN-ELEVEN GUY? WAS HE THE ONE I KICKED?
MIR
RANC
GAH!
WH-WHO'RE THEY?!
SINCE YOU ANDROIDS DON'T HAVE CHI.
YOU SURE YOU EVEN NEED US, PICCOLO?
YEAH, YOU'RE THE ONLY ONES WHO CAN FINISH THIS FIGHT.
WEIRD. SEEMS PRETTY WEAK TO ME.

GREAT. THAT'S A RELIEF.
NOW THEN...
MIR
OH, DUH! SEVEN-THREE CAN'T ABSORB ENERGY FROM THE ANDROIDS!!
GOOD THINKING, PICCOLO!
WHAT'S THAT MEAN?
NO CHI?
THOSE TWO WERE THRILLED WHEN THEY HEARD THEY COULD FILL IN FOR #17 AS RANGERS.
YEP. THEY'RE HAVING A BLAST OVER ON MONSTER ISLAND.
ARE GOTEN AND TRUNKS DOING OKAY, #18?
AS SOON AS WE MOP UP HERE, IT'S PAYDAY.
PLUS, CAPSULE CORP. IS GIVING US TEN MILLION ZENI TO FIGHT.
I'M NO FAN OF GANGING UP ON ENEMIES, BUT I CAN'T HAVE THEM WRECKING THE EARTH.
MIR
LET'S MAKE QUICK WORK OF THIS.
...
URGH...
LISTEN, I DON'T FIGHT FOR FREE.
DON'T PUT IT THAT WAY, #18. MAKES US SOUND LIKE MERCENARIES.

TCH... PATHETIC. THESE USELESS FOOLS COULDN'T EVEN MEET...
...MY LOW EXPECT-ATIONS OF THEM.

APOLO-GIES, LORD MORO.
IT SEEMS LIKE A WHOLE BUNCH OF TOUGH FIGHTERS GATHERED ON EARTH, SOME-HOW...
KREEK

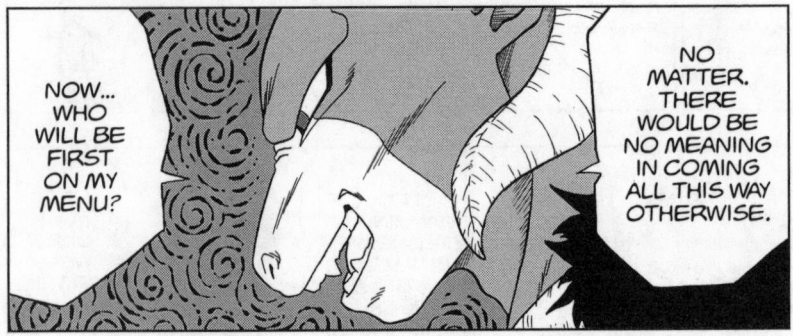
NO MATTER. THERE WOULD BE NO MEANING IN COMING ALL THIS WAY OTHERWISE.
NOW... WHO WILL BE FIRST ON MY MENU?

DAMMIT! IT FAILED...
ONE MORE TIME.

ON YAR-DRAT
HFF!
HFF!

YES. THE FIGHTING STARTED NOT LONG AGO.
CAN YOU FEEL THE EARTH'S SPIRIT?
WAIT, VEGETA.
WELL? SHOULDN'T YOU RUSH OVER THERE?
NO POINT... NOT UNTIL I'VE MASTERED THIS TECHNIQUE...
NOW! ONCE MORE!
FROM THE TOP, PYBARA.
IT'S ELDER! ELDER PYBARA!
CUTTING IT CLOSE, HUH?
THERE'S STILL TIME.
BESIDES, MORO HASN'T JOINED THE BATTLE, YET.
MEANWHILE, GOKU...
WHICH WAY IS EARTH?
THATAWAY.
...WAS A BIT LOST.
TO BE CONTINUED!

WHAT NOW? GO ON, SPIT IT OUT.

LORD FREEZA!
LORD FREEZA!
AT THAT MOMENT, SOME-WHERE DEEP IN SPACE
BONUS MANGA

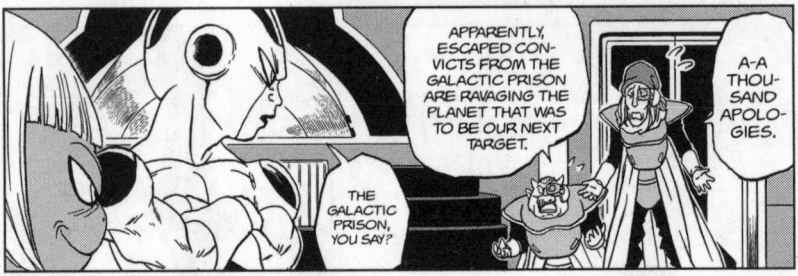
APPARENTLY, ESCAPED CON-VICTS FROM THE GALACTIC PRISON ARE RAVAGING THE PLANET THAT WAS TO BE OUR NEXT TARGET.
A-A THOU-SAND APOLO-GIES.
THE GALACTIC PRISON, YOU SAY?

NOTHING GOOD CAN COME FROM MIXING WITH CRIMINALS.
C-CRIMI-NALS ...?

...ALSO CRIMI-NALS...?
UM, AREN'T WE...

LET'S AVOID MEANINGLESS CONFLICT FOR NOW AND SIMPLY MOVE ON TO THE NEXT PLANET.
VERY WELL.

I HAVE HEARD THAT THE PRISONERS INCARCER-ATED THERE ARE AS NASTY AS THEY COME.
N-NASTY PRISONERS, LORD FREEZA?

PRECISELY AS BERRY-BLUE SAYS.
!
WE OCCUPY PLANETS AND EXTERMINATE THEIR INHABITANTS IN ORDER TO SELL THOSE PLANETS FOR A TIDY PROFIT TO RACES WHO HAVE LOST THEIR OWN HOMES.
WE ARE RUNNING A BUSINESS.
WHAT DID YOU SAY?
KIKONO, WE ARE MOST CERTAINLY NOT CRIMINALS.
ACK... NOTHING. NEVER MIND.
IT'S A BIG UNIVERSE, OUT THERE.
THEN GET SEARCHING FOR OTHER PLANETS.
Y-YES, LORD FREEZA.
IS THAT A PROBLEM, KIKONO?
NOPE!
N...

END

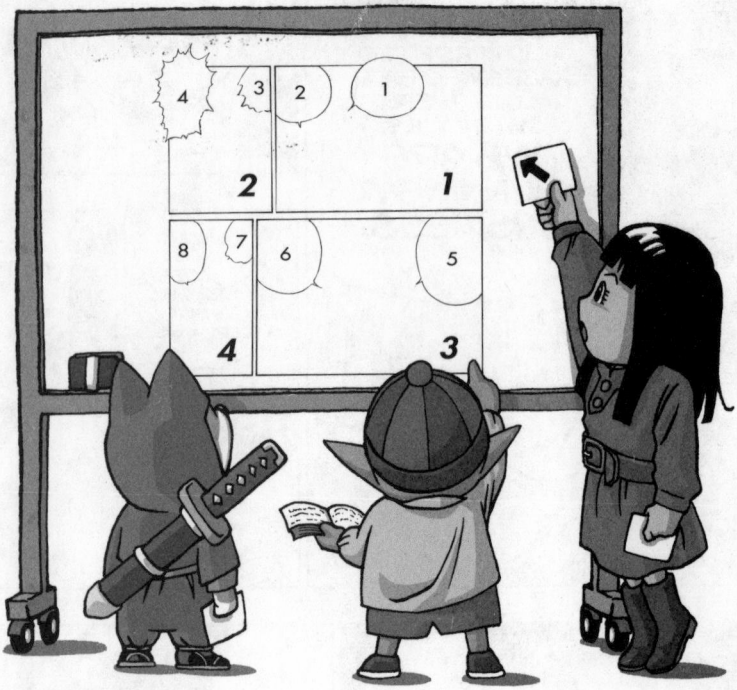

YOU'RE READING THE WRONG WAY!

Dragon Ball Super reads from right to left, starting in the upper-right corner. Japanese is read from right to left, meaning that action, sound effects, and word-balloon order are completely reversed from English order.